Praise for
How to Pay for College When You're Broke

"There's a student loan crisis looming in the United States. With stagnant wages and rising costs of education, finding alternative ways to pay for college is crucial for the next generation of college students. Jessica understands this and outlines a blueprint that helps students—and the people who care about them—understand their options."

—Tonya Rapley
CEO, My Fab Finance & The Not Just For Profit

"Knowledge is indeed power. Jessica Brown's book is a great, empowering tool for young people looking to understand how to afford, and make the most important investment, of their lives."

—Cornell Belcher
President, Brilliant Corners Research & Strategies

How to Pay for College When You're Broke

The Ultimate Guide for Students & Families
to Finance a Post-secondary Education

By Jessica L. Brown

Founder and CEO of College Gurl™

www.collegegurl.com

How to Pay for College When You're Broke: The Ultimate Guide for Students & Families to Finance a Post-secondary Education

Published by College Gurl Publishing
P.O. Box 43783
Washington, D.C. 20010

Printed in the United States of America

ISBN-13: 978-0-692-68281-4

Cover design by: Carla J. Brooks

Library of Congress Control Number: 2016914527

DISCLAIMER AND/OR LEGAL NOTICES
While the publisher and author have used their best efforts in preparing this book, they make no representations or warranties with respect to the accuracy or completeness of the contents of this book. The advice and strategies contained herein may not be suitable for your situation. You should consult a professional where appropriate. Neither the publisher nor the author shall be liable for any loss of profit or any other commercial damages, including but not limited to special, incidental, consequential, or other damages. The purchaser or reader of this publication assumes responsibility for the use of these materials and information. Adherence to all applicable laws and regulations, both advertising and all other aspects of doing business in the United States or any other jurisdiction, is the sole responsibility of the purchaser or reader.

To Tazo, thanks for giving me unconditional love.

To my family. Thank you for always believing in me and
supporting me through everything.

Jamal, thanks for giving me strength.

To Pastor Soaries and the dfree® team,
thank you for giving me a platform
to educate students and families.

Thanks to all the friends, donors, and enthusiasts
for supporting me and this project.

Lastly, to my inner self: Never stop believing in you.

Contents

4. OPPORTUNITIES AWAIT: GRANTS AND SCHOLARSHIPS 37

PART 3
NAVIGATING THE JUNGLE OF STUDENT LOANS

5. ADVANTAGES AND OPTIONS: FEDERAL STUDENT LOANS............55

6. STILL MORE POSSIBILITIES: PRIVATE STUDENT LOANS 65

7. PUTTING IT ALL TOGETHER 69

Part 1
Abundant Options

1. New Parents: Envision Your Newborn in a Mortarboard and Tassel

Experts predict that by the year 2020, 35 percent of jobs will require a bachelor's degree, minimum. The U.S. Census Bureau estimates that students who have a bachelor's degree will "earn on average $2.1 million in a lifetime—about one-third more than workers who did not finish college, and nearly twice as much as workers with only a high school diploma" (https://www.census.gov/prod/2002pubs/p23-210.pdf).

Throughout my career as a financial aid professional, I've spoken with thousands of parents who have regretted not saving early for college. They've ended up feeling guilty for being unable to afford most post-secondary (post-high school) educational institutions.

No parent wants to tell their child that they cannot afford their dream school, the school that would lead to a career their child would excel in and profit from throughout life. This is why you must plan early and start saving for your child's college education today.

Many new parents decide they'll look into it "later." After all, they have seventeen or eighteen years. Unfortunately, "later" goes by in a blink.

Consider this. How America Pays for College, a national study conducted by Sallie Mae, shows that undergraduate students and their parents spent an average of $24,164 on college in the 2014-2015 academic year. This number jumped 16 percent from the previous year. And that number continues to rise.

How America *Saves* (emphasis added) for College "found that while families overwhelmingly believe college is an investment for their children, fewer than half of families are saving for college, and the amount of money they are saving for college is less than last year" (https://www.salliemae.com/plan-for-college/how-america-saves-for-college/?dtd_cell=SMPLCADCOTDOWBOTO THOTHRR010022).

I have an older sister who went to college four years before me. Even though my parents are no longer together, they had to sit down and figure out how they would collectively pay for college for eight consecutive years. Our house rule was you had to go out of state for college at least for the first two years. So, my sister attended Pennsylvania State University for two years and Rutgers University her last two years. Pennsylvania State University cost my parents about $90,000, including costs of travel, living expenses, and spending money.

Once the economy began to decline, so did my parents' lucrative careers. By the time I went to college, finances became strained. My dad's business started to decline at the same time my college bills were coming in. My mother did everything in her power to try and pay for my next four years, but the economy gradually won the battle. I had to work hard to afford to stay in college.

Paying for your child's post-secondary education is one of the largest investments of your lifetime. You need to be realistic and set aside a portion of every paycheck to contribute to your child's education. When you do, paying for college will be much easier.

It's understandable that you want the best for your child and are willing to sacrifice for it, yet you should fully realize how that will impact your financial future—especially if you have two or more children who will eventually attend college.

With that in mind, let's start helping you save for your child's college education.

In order to see where you stand financially so you know how much to set aside, make a detailed list of your:

- annual income
- retirement accounts
- savings
- investment accounts
- monthly expenses

Once you analyze these items, you will see where your money goes every month and will be able to evaluate how much of each paycheck you can set aside for college. Knowing the average cost is $24,164 per year, we can reasonably assume each academic year will cost $30,000 or more in eighteen years. So $30,000, divided by 18 years, means you should set aside $1,667 each year, or $140 per month, for each year of college you will need to afford.

If you do not review your finances properly and start saving now, you may take out loans in eighteen years, though that may impact your personal financial goals *or* put you and/or your child in thousands of dollars of debt postcollege.

Now, as this book's title indicates, many of us are paying this month's bills with last month's check or have no income at all. This makes it difficult when trying to contribute to your child's education.

But families can't heavily rely on the government and prospective schools for enough money to cover the Cost of Attendance. Instead, we have to do what it takes to get out of debt and start saving.

According to Dr. Deforest Soaries, author of *dfree: Breaking Free from Financial Slavery*, "We must learn to replace the harmful ingredients in the culture of debt with life-giving agents of clarity, freedom, and responsibility. The beginning of this process is to face the reality of your situation, one step at a time, one day at a time. For many people who deliberately keep their heads in the sand to avoid the painful reality of their financial slavery, it's going to require more courage than education. For others who are enthusiastic about taking control of their financial responsibilities, the process may be more about learning some basics than unraveling motives."

In the following sections, parents will find good savings options for their child's future college education.

- Savings Accounts
- U.S. EE Savings Bonds
- 529 Plans
- Educational IRAs

Savings Accounts

Opening a savings account early on can greatly help with college expenses. It can also minimize the stress on your family.

College funds might not be able to cover all four years at a traditional institution, and maybe not even the first year, but anything helps.

✓ Open a regular bank savings account that allows you and your child to save together. Teaching yourself and your child to deposit instead of withdraw funds is imperative for financial security and success.

U.S. EE Savings Bonds

As a child you may have collected savings bonds from contests, birthdays, or as a token of love from your grandparents. When you first received a bond, you might have not understood the importance. However, EE savings bonds are a great way to save for you and/or your child's education.

Over time these bonds can accumulate to be worth hundreds or thousands of dollars. EE savings bonds have a fixed interest rate for up to thirty years. The interest rate is set, once you purchase the bond. The minimum purchase for an EE savings bond is $25.

If you're interested in this low-risk way to save money, you may purchase savings bonds online directly from the U.S. Treasury at http://treasurydirect.gov/. Paper bonds are no longer issued, therefore you must purchase EE bonds online.

Once you have purchased a bond, you must register it so that the government knows who owns the bond and who can cash it (https://www.treasurydirect.gov/indiv/research/indepth/ ebonds/ res_e_bonds_eebuy.htm). You may also track how much the bond is worth throughout the years by using online savings bonds calculators.

529 Plans

A 529 plan is a popular method of saving money. It's an educational savings plan operated by individual states and educational institutions.

All the interests and earnings you accrue in the 529 are tax-free as long as you use the funds toward your child's education. If you withdraw the money for a purpose other than college expenses, you may be penalized.

(It was so named since it was sanctioned by Section 529 of the Internal Revenue Code. It's also known as a "qualified tuition plan.")

Available are two types of 529 plans, the 529 Prepaid Tuition Plan and the 529 College Savings Plan.

529 Prepaid Tuition Plan

As stated by http://www.finaid.org/savings/529plans.phtml, "Prepaid tuition plans are college savings plans that are guaranteed to increase in value at the same rate as college tuition. For example, if a family purchases shares worth half a year's tuition at a state college, these shares will always be worth half a year's tuition—even ten years later, when tuition rates may have doubled.

The main benefit of these plans is that they allow a student's parents to lock in tuition at current rates, offering peace of mind. The plans' simplicity is also attractive, and most offer a better rate of return on an investment than bank savings accounts and certificates of deposit. The plans also involve no risk to principal, and often are guaranteed by the full faith and credit of the state."

If you're interested in having this 529 plan, you must have a beneficiary (child) assigned to it, and the beneficiary has to be enrolled in a post-secondary educational program.

If one of your children doesn't go to college, you can transfer the money to another child or close relative who is going to college. No matter who you assign as a beneficiary, you will always be in control of the money.

529 College Savings Plan

The website http://www.finaid.org/savings/529plans.phtml also explains, "Section 529 college savings plans are tax-exempt college savings vehicles with a low impact on need-based financial aid eligibility. Unlike prepaid tuition plans, there is no lock on tuition rates and no guarantee. Investments are subject to market conditions, and the savings may not be sufficient to cover all college costs. However, with this added risk comes the opportunity for potentially earning greater returns.

Most 529 college savings plans offer an adaptive asset allocation strategy based on the age of the child or the number of years until enrollment. These plans start off aggressively when the child is younger, and gradually switch to more conservative investments as college approaches. Typically they will use four or five age ranges, such as newborn-6, 7-9, 10-12, 13-15, and 16-18+."

There is no age limitation on 529 and no maximum amount you can contribute.

However, 529s may only be used for higher public education, not private schools. Also, they may impact your child's need-based aid and/or *institutional* aid. So it's important to check with the financial aid office of the college your child is likely to attend about their policies and procedures around the 529 plan.

Lastly, it is never too early to enroll in a 529 plan. Before applying for a 529, speak with a financial advisor to see if this option is good for you.

If it is a good option, keep in mind that the earlier you start, the more you will save up.

Educational IRAs

Educational IRAs work similar to the 529, yet there are some differences.

- Account holders may deposit only $2,000 per year per child.
- The growth of earnings is not taxed until the funds are withdrawn.
- These funds can be used for private schools, including grades 1-12, and for higher education.
- Money is not counted toward student aid.
- An Educational IRA has age limitations. All funds must be used by the beneficiary by the time he or she is thirty.

The website http://www.ira-basics.com/what-is-an-educational-ira/ clarifies, "You make after-tax contributions to the plans and all earnings or capital gains accumulate tax deferred. Then, if you make withdrawals to pay for higher education, the withdrawals are totally tax free. Costs include tuition, books, fees, room, board, laptop, and even cell phones."

2. High School Parents and Students: Choices for Post-High-School Education

The Plan

The first step in seeking a postsecondary education is financial planning. College may be an exciting time, yet it may also be a daunting one if you do not have the funds to pay for it.

Schools today want to know how you plan to finance each year before it begins. Some have begun making families pay up in full before classes start. To reduce debt and unpaid balances, many are now requesting that, prior to every semester, students provide a financial plan that includes how they are planning to finance their education outside of the amounts awarded to them from the school. If they do not see you have resources secured, you may be unable to attend. Schools do not have time to wait and figure out how you plan to pay.

Making a to-do list is a great way to get organized and follow up on potential opportunities. Applying to college can be a tedious, hectic, and time-consuming process. Yet keeping track of what you and/or your child need to do to secure funds is important to your financial security. Your to-do list should include researching schools you're interested in, their Cost of Attendance, location, and scholarship opportunities. Then you can determine if you'll be able to afford the school, and if not, how you plan to make up the shortfall.

Ideally, you want to begin planning as early as possible. Many students and families aren't aware of how much a college education costs annually, and costs keep going up. It is an unfortunate fact that the cost of living is increasing across the world and families aren't seeing an increase in pay. That makes saving for a child's college tuition difficult.

Yet, waiting until the ninth hour to scramble to find ways to pay for college can be very stressful and unpredictable. So time is of the essence.

Sit down as a family. Ask your teen what their interests and career goals are and what they want out of a college education. Know if the major they choose is going to be a good fit for them and provide them a lucrative career.

Next, ask yourself how much can you contribute annually to your teen's choices. Create a blueprint of your current financial status to help you. Make a detailed list of your:

- annual income
- retirement accounts
- savings and investment accounts
- monthly bills (i.e., car note, insurance, mortgage/rent, utilities, etc.)

Also, list all factors that are important to you and your family, such as your personal financial goals.

From the remaining funds, decide how much you want to invest in your teen's postsecondary education. Other financial aid may be available (I'll discuss options in upcoming chapters), but for now keep your chosen investment amount in mind to help you narrow down your college search.

Is a pricey four-year university your only option? Not at all. Even though the cost of tuition is rising annually, some colleges are more affordable than you might think, though you may need to pick a school and program where you and your family can pay the out-of-pocket expenses. In the sections just ahead are possibilities to consider other than a pricey four-year. But the search begins with one all-important question:

Is this institution affordable for us?

Affordability is key in securing a post-secondary education. We all want to attend the most reputable school, yet that may not be financially feasible. Don't underestimate your education because of the price. Educational institutions across the world come with experiences and knowledge important to your future career. The name and price of the school do *not* define the education that it can provide you.

Pride will make you feel as if you can afford everything, when in reality you can't. Do not feel like you have to impress others with the name of your college. An education is an education; it is not where you go but what you make out of it.

So be realistic with yourself and situation and ask yourself, Is this affordable?

Research all your educational options. Look into schools that may not be your first choice.

Once you complete your research, check and see which option is more affordable for you. Be sure to think about the future beforehand to know if your decision is the right one for you.

Following are types of educational institutions for you to consider.

Community College

For some students coming out of high school, attending a four-year university can be intimidating . . . and expensive. You can save thousands of dollars by living at home and taking courses at a nearby community college.

Community colleges have a few outstanding advantages: Class sizes are smaller so you have a better teacher-to-student ratio, and you'll have more flexible class schedules. Flexible schedules allow you to work and earn money while still getting an education. Many traditional four-year schools don't have flexible class schedules or online courses, which can make earning money and taking care of responsibilities during college difficult.

A lot of community college courses are transferrable to four-year universities, putting you on a smooth track to earning your bachelor's degree. If you are interested in attending a four-year school after community college:

✓ Be sure to review programs that will transfer to your four-year university, and ensure all credits will transfer.

Some careers don't require you to get a bachelor's degree, but many do. Before going to school, research potential careers. You might discover that the career you want does not require any post-secondary education, or that it simply requires an associate degree or certain classes completed. Research prospective careers to find out what yours requires.

If your career doesn't require a bachelor's degree, then community college may be a perfect fit.

Note: Even though it's cost effective to attend a community college, research shows that many students who attend *only* community college have more issues with paying back their loans. The issue stems from students not earning a degree and having to accept a job that does not offer enough money to pay the loans back.

David Baime, a senior policy expert at the American Association of Community Colleges says, "The less you borrow, the likelier you are to default, and that is very much a community college phenomenon" (http://finance.yahoo.com/news/community-college-problems-162559087.html).

Students who attend a four-year institution have a higher repayment rate than community and for-profit schools, because they are securing high paying careers. Therefore, it is important to research all careers you are interested in to see which path is best for you.

For-Profit and Trade Schools: Are They Worth the Money?

There's a saying that serving profit and the public good can be a conflict of interest. So, when considering a for-profit college for your education, you must know if this is the best option for you.

What is a for-profit college? It's a school that is owned and operated by a private business or investors, a business that wants to profit by offering students an education. Many of these schools seek out students who are older and trying to get back into school. These schools' admissions departments have quotas to meet and will do anything to make those numbers. That means they will enroll you and tell you all sorts of great things but often let you fall by the wayside during your matriculation.

What is a trade school? A trade school (aka vocational school) teaches students a specific trade or career.

As noted by http://www.thesimpledollar.com/why-you-should-consider-trade-school-instead-of-college/, "Trade schools are a more streamlined approach to education, with curricula focusing on developing a particular skillset and knowledge base for a career rather than receiving a general education. Trade schools typically take a lot less time to complete, have smaller class sizes, and the majority of the training is hands-on, which is an ideal environment for many types of learners."

With either a for-profit or a trade school, graduates become plumbers, electricians, auto mechanics, computer programmers, chefs, cosmetologists, travel agents, dental hygienists, and more, depending on which career field a school specializes in.

Since these schools earn a profit, maybe you can already see potential problems here, including quality of education and cost.

Research Student Reviews

The fastest way to thoroughly research a for-profit or trade school (or any other school) is to go straight to present and former students' reviews—and their comments—online.

✓ Simply search the keywords "[school's name]" and "reviews."

If you see an abundance of low and negative reviews, skip all the steps below and research a different school.

You can also ask current students of your preferred for-profit college or trade school, "Does this college's (school's) programs really enforce education, or does the college (school) let you fall by the wayside after they deposit your check?"

Research the College's or School's Revenue

According to writer Lindsay Haskell, "The average tuition at a for-profit college is six times higher than a community college and twice as high as a public four-year school" (http://www.ocregister.com/taxdollars/strong-478859-percent-four.html). That's huge! You should check the revenue that the school you are considering brings in annually. Some for-profit and trade schools' earnings in recent years has been in the *billions*.

Some of these schools intentionally recruit low-income students since they get the most in federal Pell Grants and loans.

As you research each school and related reviews, objectively ask yourself, "Is this school worth the price?"

Verify Written and Orally Stated "Facts"

Once you sign up to receive information from a for-profit or trade school, they will continuously call and follow up to get you in to see the campus and programs.

For-profit and trade schools' admission counselors are required to meet goals. After you enroll, many will not be as attentive to you as when you were a prospective student.

Typically the school's sales pitch is, "Our school will give you the skills you need to get a good paying job without enrolling in a traditional institution." This might be true. It also may be misleading or false.

If you don't want to spend the next four years of your life in a classroom, then a trade/for-profit school may be beneficial to you. Keep in mind there are many careers that don't require a four-year degree. Trade schools offer flexible options but tend to have high student turnover rates.

✓ Research community colleges with the same program and see if the price and curriculum work for you.

If you continue to have interest in a for-profit or trade school, pay attention to what is said and implied. It's easier to convince a single mother of two to enroll in a for-profit or trade school because then she can jump into a career "fast." Yet they do not tell you that you'll still be up against dozens of your fellow graduates and other people all trying to get the same job as you are.

Don't let the oral or written advertising of these schools entice you into thinking that you will land that big job immediately after graduation. Ask if their career services team will help set you up with an employer postgraduation. Many schools do offer this feature, so it's important to take advantage, though be sure this is part of the signed agreement.

Research Graduation Rates

Since many for-profit institutions have high student turnover rates, research the graduation rates of these institutions. If you see that the graduation rates and opportunities are not to your standards, do not invest.

Take Your Time

If you decide to apply, take your time. Understand what you are signing when you go into these for-profit/trade schools' admissions offices. They will have financial aid reps, teachers, and directors all welcoming you at once, and before you know it, you've enrolled. You didn't get the opportunity to say "no" or "let me sleep on it." These counselors are not just there to help; they are trying to sell. Some lie and say that you will make xyz dollars to get you more intrigued and use psychological tactics to get you to sign on the dotted line.

They will tell you how they are so affordable that you will still receive a refund. (Refunds stem from an excess of student loans or aid to your account. If you have an overflow of money coming in to pay off your bill, you may be eligible for a refund. Many students may get refunds from student loans, which they are supposed to use for educational expenses. Yet, many of them utilize them for other expenses outside of educational expenses.)

What counselors will *not* tell you is that these refunds continuously pile up, leading to more student loan debt, making payments postcollege unbearable to maintain.

In my tenure, I've seen admissions representatives not allow you to speak with financial aid until they're confident you'll sign up. You should have the opportunity to speak with a representative to understand your potential package prior to enrolling.

Schools may over-promise what they can do for you, and before you know it, you're stuck paying the loan servicers back for the time you spent and did not even finish.

Do your research.

Four-Year Colleges: Research on Campus

Much of the research you would do when considering a for-profit or trade school you should also do if you want to attend a four-year college. However, this traditional college option requires another layer of investigation.

Many students and families prefer to go to four-year colleges far away from home. As a result, they spend thousands in travel expenses to visit prospective campuses. You can save money by eliminating the number of on-campus tours by using virtual campus tours by visiting college websites. (Remain mindful of travel, since this can be a costly expense, especially when you want to go home for holidays.) Virtual tours allow you to minimize the number of schools you'll visit in person.

When visiting a school, it's important to ask yourself if you can see yourself in that environment. Don't be pressured to pay because of a college visit. You're investing your time and money into these next few years, so choose your profession and school wisely.

Many places make you take out loans just for certifications that don't take you far. Link up with counselors and campus directors to understand the opportunities that these schools can give you. Don't be shy—this is your money and your time.

Please note: State universities have different rates for in-state and out-of-state students. Rates for in-state students are more affordable. However, in-state and out-of-state rates don't matter when applying to private institutions. Therefore, be sure to understand the rates and which rate applies to your situation.

Dual Enrollment Programs

High school students may be eligible to participate in dual enrollment programs, where they can take college courses at local universities or community colleges for both college and high school credit.

These programs are designed to help jump-start students' college career and enhance their academic performance. This opportunity also provides students helpful exposure to the college environment.

Many local universities partner with high schools to give students the opportunity to earn credit that can be transferred to any post-secondary institution.

These programs are typically funded by the state and cover the student's tuition, fees, and books.

Many of these dual enrollment programs are available for free. This cost-saving measure will help kick off your college career and save money. Therefore, please check with your guidance counselors and local institutions to see if you may utilize this benefit.

Part 2
College Financial Aid Options to Help You Reach the Cap and Gown

3. Financial Aid: It All Begins with FAFSA

What is Financial Aid?

Financial aid is the financial assistance that helps you pay for college tuition. It is made up of loans, scholarships, and/or grants, which are forms of self-help or need-based aid.

Money that you receive through a loan must be paid back. Scholarships and grants are known as "gift aid," because it is money that you do not have to pay back.

"Merit-based aid" is based on academic performance or skill set. In other words, you must retain a certain level of performance in order to be (and remain) eligible for this form of financial assistance.

Also, if the Free Application of Federal Student Aid (FAFSA) determines you are financially needy, you may be eligible for additional grants. **Financially needy** is a term that is used by the U.S. Department of Education to determine a family's financial need, which is based on income, family size, and similar factors.

More than $185 billion dollars in financial aid is available to help pay for college. That includes monies from federal and state governments, universities, and private organizations (https://www.amherst.edu/system/files/media/General%2520 Financial%2520Aid%2520Information.pdf).

FAFSA

Completing the Free Application for Federal Student Aid (FAFSA) is one of the first steps in seeking a post-secondary education. It is a key first step because you need to see where you financially stand in order to learn what aid you may be eligible for. The result of the FAFSA might change the school you attend, since the amount awarded to pay for education is based on the information you provide.

The FAFSA helps determine the awarding of over $150 billion dollars annually in grants, work-study funds, and as low-interest loans (https://fafsa.ed.gov/fotw1617/help/typesof Aid.htm).

Throughout my tenure as a financial aid professional, I've met students and parents who do not fill out the FAFSA because they don't feel they will qualify for anything. However, they are frequently mistaken! You should still fill out a FAFSA even if you and your family are in a good financial situation. Even if you have the means, you'll never know what aid you can be eligible for that may be provided by the government, state, or prospective school.

You may be eligible for institutional aid that might not disburse if there is no FAFSA on file for you.

What Do I Need in Order to Fill Out the FAFSA?

"You will need:

- your social security number
- your alien registration number (if you are not a U.S. citizen)
- your most recent federal income tax returns, W-2s, and other records of money earned

- bank statements and records of investments (if applicable)
- records of untaxed income (if applicable)
- a FSA ID to sign electronically" (https://fafsa.ed.gov/help/before003.htm).

You must accurately fill out your information *and* accurately report your tax data on the FAFSA. Some people believe that if they lower their income they might receive more in financial aid, which is not true.

If you do not accurately report your information, you may be subject to verification. Verification will confirm whether the information you submitted is correct. If it is not correct, your financial aid package may be delayed and possibly denied.

According to the U.S. Department of Education, "If you receive federal student aid based on incorrect or fraudulent information, you will have to pay it back. You may also have to pay fines and fees. If you purposely provide false or misleading information on the FAFSA, you may be fined up to $20,000, sent to prison, or both" (https://fafsa.ed.gov/help/fftoc06b.htm).

Therefore, it is critical to provide accurate information.

Create a FSA ID

The FSA ID will be your first step in accessing the FAFSA. You will not be able to complete your financial aid process without it.

(Parent, both you and your child need a FSA ID in order to complete the FAFSA . . . if you are a parent of a *dependent* post-secondary student.) Your FSA ID will enable you to electronically sign the FAFSA; it is your legal signature and should *only* be used by the owner.

Ensuring you enter the correct information is crucial! Information must match exactly, so please be certain you do not have any errors before submission. You would hate to have potential problems in the future.

You'll need to remember this ID for as long as you and/or your child is in college. If you are having log in issues, be sure to contact the Federal Student Aid Information Center at 1(800) 433-3243.

The FSA ID can be used on all U.S. Department of Education websites such as https://fafsa.ed.gov/, https://www.nslds.ed.gov/nslds/nslds_SA/, https://studentaid.ed.gov/sa/, and https://teach-ats.ed.gov/ats/index.action. Once your FSA ID is created, you will have access to complete the FAFSA and its requirements.

You can create your FSA ID anytime.

✓ Create your FSA ID at https://fsaid.ed.gov/npas/ index.htm.

Dependency Status

When you fill out the FAFSA (do this at https://fafsa.ed.gov/), you will be asked to provide your dependency status. "Dependency" means who claims you on their taxes. For example, do your parents claim you on their taxes as their dependent?

Your dependency status is important because it will impact your college funding.

Dependency status determines whose information you have to report on your FAFSA. If you are a dependent student, you will report your and your parents' or guardians' income. If your parents are divorced, use the taxes of the parent who is claiming you on their return (it's likely the parent you have lived with for more than six months).

If you are an independent student, you will only report your own income, and your spouse's, if you are married (https://studentaid.ed.gov/sa/fafsa/filling-out/dependency).

Dependency status will be based on your answers to questions 46 to 58 on the FAFSA.

Just because you file your own taxes doesn't mean you are an independent student. Many students believe they're independent because they just got their first apartment, claimed residency in a new state, or filed taxes on their own. Yet, dependency status is based on answering "yes" to one or more of the questions listed below. If you answer yes to any of these questions, you will not need to supply your parents' tax information to complete the FAFSA. You will be considered independent.

Your Dependency Status

Are you:

- born before January 1, 1993?
- married?
- working toward a doctorate or master's program?
- currently serving in the U.S. armed forces on active duty (and not solely in training)?
- a U.S. armed forces veteran?
- Do you have—or will have—children who will get half or more of their support from you between July 1 of

this year, and June 30 of next year?

- Other than your spouse and children, do you have dependents who live with you and who get half or more of their support from you, between now and through June 30 of next year?
- Since the age of thirteen, were you at any time a child of two deceased parents, in foster care, or a court dependent or ward?
- "An emancipated minor or that someone other than your parent or stepparent has legal guardianship of you? (You also should answer 'yes' if you are now an adult but were in legal guardianship immediately before you reached the age of being an adult in your state. Answer 'no' if the court papers say 'custody' rather than 'guardianship.')"
- "At any time on or after July 1, 2015, were you determined to be an unaccompanied youth who was homeless or were self-supporting and at risk of being homeless, as determined by (a) your high school or district homeless liaison, (b) the director of an emergency shelter or transitional housing program funded by the U.S. Department of Housing and Urban Development, or (c) the director of a runaway or homeless youth basic center or transitional living program?"

(The above is based on or, if enclosed in quotation marks, quoted from the questionnaire at www.studentaid.ed.gov/ sa/fafsa/filling-out/dependency #dependent-or-independent.)

Again, if you answer yes to one or more of the above questions, that will determine your dependency status, which in turn will determine your loan amount eligibility.

Tax Information

As mentioned above, in order to complete the FAFSA you need to provide the most current tax information. If you or your parents haven't filed for the most recent year, you may use the previous year's taxes until you file for the current year. However, you must make a FAFSA correction once your recent year's taxes are complete.

If you have completed your taxes, you can electronically link and auto-fill your tax information by using the handy IRS Data Retrieval Tool (DRT).

This is an excellent tool to use, because it quickly ensures that all your tax information is accurate. The tax information is the most intricate (tedious) part of the process . . . *if* you enter the figures manually. Using the Data Retrieval Tool helps ensure fast data entry and that you receive exactly the right amount of financial aid.

(Data Retrieval Tool and related terms are capitalized in this book since they are capitalized terms you will encounter during the financial aid process.)

The information represented in the tax information will help determine your Expected Family Contribution (EFC). This is the annual amount that the government expects you and your parent(s) to be able to pay toward your college education.

The Cost of Attendance (COA) – Family Contributions
= Financial Need

Cost of Attendance includes tuition, room and board, fees, books, supplies, transportation, and personal expenses. Family Contributions are your and/or parents' incomes and spouses' incomes. Once these factors are subtracted, it will equal your financial need.

The italicized equation above determines if the Cost of Attendance exceeds your calculated Expected Family Contribution. If it does, you will be eligible for need-based **grants** and/or **loans** to help pay for your educational expenses. (I'll discuss grants, loans, and similar types of financial aid in detail shortly.)

There are some parents who are not in contact with their children. As a result, they will not supply them with any information. If you are in this situation, you will need to call the U.S. Department of Education and your school's financial aid office to see what information you may need to supply to prove that you do not have contact with your parent(s), and to learn how to proceed.

Household Size

Parents and students might say the Expected Family Contribution is not a correct representation of their household. For example, if a parent makes $150,000 and has two kids, you may not be eligible for a grant because the government may not see a strong financial need.

Critics of the above formula may say you cannot judge a household because of the income. Just because you make over a certain amount does not mean you can contribute to your child's education. However, this is the formula the federal government uses to determine aid. Therefore, it is imperative to ensure that your child is seeking alternative methods of payment for college, such as grants, scholarships, internships, subsidized loans, and unsubsidized loans (discussed shortly). However, those alternative methods of payment might not be enough to cover a full year of tuition at a traditional institution.

Yet, if you have ten people within the household with the same income, you may be eligible for additional funding.

Income and household size play an important role in aid eligibility and determining a family's financial need. Schools and the results from the FAFSA determine the award a student should receive.

Divorced, Single Parent, or Getting Married? How It Affects FAFSA Financial Aid

If you or your parents have divorced, understand whose information to put on the FAFSA.

Are you a future college student's parent in the process of divorce? Be sure to add educational expenses to your divorce papers. This will ensure your child's education is secure.

Are you a future college student whose parents have divorced? Then you must put in the parent that you most recently lived with within the last twelve months, which is most likely the parent who claimed you on their taxes.

In some instances, schools may provide additional funding for children of divorce or single-parent households, especially if the child lives with the lower income parent.

As a single parent, it may be difficult to contribute to your child's educational expenses. Know that some single-parent households qualify for more since there is only one income. (Note that FAFSA financial aid depends on annual income and household size.)

If you are getting married and have a child prior to the marriage, the new spouse's income will have to be listed on the

FAFSA. However, if you get married after the FAFSA has already been submitted for that year, then you don't have to go back in and make a correction. (Note that in the years following, you will have to add the new spouse's information on your FAFSA, since his or her information will be added to your tax information. This may disqualify you from receiving additional funds, as you are no longer a single parent.)

When filing your taxes, you will have to list both incomes as well as the children within your household, meaning that the new parent's income will affect the Expected Family Contribution.

FAFSA and the Federal Work-Study Program

When you complete the FAFSA, the results can also determine whether you may be eligible for Federal Work-Study. The Federal Work-Study (FWS) Program helps connect college students to part-time jobs (up to twenty hours per week) when they have financial need (determined by the FAFSA and Expected Family Contribution). The part-time job helps the student pay educational expenses and provides community service and/or career development, which enables them to gain valuable experience.

Note: Not all colleges participate in Federal Work-Study. Contact your school's financial aid office to learn whether they participate.

Complete a New FAFSA Each Year You Attend College

You must fill out the FAFSA annually to requalify for federal, state, and institutional aid, because the information does not roll over. Since your circumstances may change at any time, you need to report your information every year while you are in school.

You will not receive a new award package from the financial aid office until this is complete.

Fill Out the FAFSA

You can begin filing out your FAFSA as early as October 1.

In September 2015, President Obama announced a change to the FAFSA. This change allows all students and families to access the FAFSA as early as October 1. For the 2017-2018 academic year and afterward, all FAFSAs will be available on October 1, instead of three months later on January 1. This allows more time for family financial planning.

Please be aware of your state's deadline when completing the FAFSA. You may be eligible for additional aid if you complete it by the state's date.

The federal deadline for completion is June 30.

Early submission of your FAFSA will allow you to see exactly how much money you will qualify for, while giving you time to find more financial resources.

Make sure when you complete the FAFSA that you are on https://fafsa.ed.gov/! If you're on any other website besides the FAFSA, it is a third party servicer! A third party servicer is when other people fill out your application for a fee! The first word in FAFSA is *free*, and filling it out is quite simple. So please don't pay anyone to fill out your FAFSA for you!

✓ Complete the FAFSA at https://fafsa.ed.gov/.

The results from your FAFSA will be generated into your **Student Aid Report** (SAR), which will provide you information (based on your FAFSA answers) about your eligibility for federal student aid.

The results of your FAFSA will also be provided to each of the schools you apply to and will inform them of your financial aid eligibility.

4. Opportunities Await:
Grants and Scholarships

Pell Grant

The Federal Pell Grant is a grant that undergraduate students may be eligible for based on the information provided on the FAFSA. It is a guaranteed grant if your family is classified as financially needy. You must have an Expected Family Contribution between 0-5000 to qualify for a Pell Grant, 0 being extremely needy.

This grant is gift aid aka need-based aid. It is money that you don't have to pay back.

Federal Supplemental Educational Opportunity Grant (FSEOG)

Like the Pell Grant, FSEOG is determined by the FAFSA. Both grants are provided by the federal government to low-income households with a strong financial need.

Unlike the Pell, this grant is not guaranteed to everyone since federal funds are limited. Therefore, it is important to submit your FAFSA early to qualify.

Please note that not all schools provide FSEOG, so it is imperative to speak with your prospective financial aid office about this grant option.

Scholarships

Did you know that last year 100 million dollars in scholarship funds go unclaimed? That means a lot more students across the country could be researching and benefitting from scholarship opportunities.

According to Merriam Webster, a scholarship is "an amount of money that is given by a school, an organization, etc., to a student to help pay for the student's education" (http://www.merriam-webster.com/dictionary/scholarship). Like the Pell Grant, a scholarship is gift aid. It is money that you don't have to pay back.

Scholarships help defray educational costs and allow you to focus on the task at hand—school. As much time as you spend on social media seeing "what's popping," you could be researching opportunities that will help your future.

I cannot stress enough the importance of researching and completing scholarships. Many students would not be in college if it weren't for scholarships.

Locate Scholarships Online

You can find thousands of scholarships online. Some are discipline (field of study) related, yet there are many for students of all interests.

Utilizing scholarship search engines, apps, and websites will help with your search.

- ✓ Fastweb, Cappex, CollegeBoard, and Scholarships.com® are a few of the best means to find scholarships.

Once you create a free profile on these sites, they will send you scholarships that fit your profile.

Be aware of scams! Many websites try to make you pay to see which scholarships are available. You should never have to pay to view scholarships . . . with *one* exception.

There's a new app developed by Drexel student Christopher Gray called Scholly, which can be purchased for 99 cents. "Scholly connects students and families with the best scholarship matches, fast, because we know that student success starts with affording college" (http://home.myscholly.com/#scholly).

Gray created this app because he received one million dollars in scholarships and has quickly become known as the "Million Dollar Scholar." After pitching this on *Shark Tank* in 2014, Scholly became one of the top apps purchased on iTunes in 2015.

This app makes it easy to find scholarships on your mobile phone within seconds!

Kinds of Scholarships
MERIT (ACADEMIC) SCHOLARSHIPS

Merit scholarships (aka academic scholarships) are scholarships given to students based on previous school performance. These scholarships are usually provided by the college or institution and can help with some to all necessary financial aid. Many merit scholarships are available to incoming freshman students and transfer students.

Since these scholarships are awarded to students with outstanding GPA, SAT, and ACT scores and resumes, it's crucial that you academically excel throughout your educational career.

However, if you continuously take (retake) the ACTs or SATs throughout the application process, that may hinder you from meeting scholarships deadlines. Some students wait until the last minute to test, and they may miss out on potential opportunities to receive additional aid. Therefore, be sure to test early and not wait until the last minute.

To begin the process, check in with your prospective school's financial aid office to find out about scholarships available for incoming and continuing students. Ask if they have a list of scholarships within the institution and locally. This will allow you to see potential opportunities before enrolling.

Also, visit *other schools' financial aid websites*. They might have insight on more *national* scholarships that you may be eligible for. Since most schools offer merit scholarships, you should research each school's qualifications so that you might be considered, even it's a school you didn't plan on attending. You should go where the money is.

If you go on a college tour, be sure to visit schools' financial aid offices. Ask about the Cost of Attendance and potential opportunities to receive scholarships. Speaking with a financial aid advisor will give you and your family a better idea of how much an education will cost.

✓ Prior to applying, research your prospective school's scholarship eligibility requirements.

Strive to build relationships within your prospective school's financial aid office. As a financial aid professional, I've awarded hundreds of thousands of dollars to hundreds of students around the world. Some students I have never met, yet

I've communicated with them via phone or e-mail. Reach out to your school, either in person or through technology (or both). You never know what the school might offer you. Financial aid offices give out institutional aid based on need or special characteristics of a student. Yet, if you don't put in extra effort for additional funding, you may never know if the school would have given you additional funds.

There are times where financial aid offices have exhausted their funding, which is why you need to contact them in the *beginning* stages of the awarding process.

Moreover, follow up (by being persistent, but not annoying!) with the financial aid office even if they have previously told you no, because you might follow up at a time when additional funding has become available. If award packages aren't accepted by students by a certain date, financial aid offices may re-gift aid to other eligible students.

Be aware: Many students and families depend on their circumstances (i.e., low income or job loss) to receive more funding from the government and schools. You can't depend on this factor alone since funding is unpredictable. Even though your circumstance may be rough, that does not mean you will qualify for more money. Some students believe if they tell the financial aid offices of their hardship the office will provide more. Some do, but some don't. So it's important not to rely on the results from your FAFSA or the college financial aid department. If you know your circumstances are extenuating, then continue to search for scholarships.

When applying to schools, most students just call the financial aid office to see if there is additional funding available. However, if funding comes up short, it is just as important to call the school's department that you plan to attend. Many departments and schools within universities offer scholarships that students are not aware of. They receive resources from donors and external organizations annually that the financial aid office is not aware of. If you need to, call or visit your prospective department to see what other options may be available.

Most scholarships and institutional aid from universities are awarded "first come first serve." Filling out your FAFSA early will allow you to qualify for additional funds.

If the financial aid office doesn't offer you additional aid to help offset your expenses, doesn't communicate their deadline for applying, or is not responsive, then that school may not be the one for you. You want to enroll in a school that is going to provide you opportunities. Even if additional funding is not available your freshman year, you hope to secure funds in the future.

✓ For a great merit scholarship opportunity, research the Gates Millennium Scholars Program by Bill and Melinda Gates. It's for "for outstanding minority students with significant financial need" (https://www.gmsp.org/). They offer to pay all four years of college, including books!

ATHLETIC SCHOLARSHIPS

If you plan to play sports at the collegiate level, you may be eligible to receive an athletic scholarship.

However, just because you played sports in high school doesn't mean you will be awarded an athletic scholarship.

Division I and Division II schools offer athletic scholarships. Division I schools provide more in athletic aid than Division II schools. (Division III schools do not offer any athletic scholarship aid.) Therefore it is important to speak with a representative within each prospective school to see what options are available.

Athletic scholarships are based on athletic performance and are given by the prospective schools' athletic departments. These schools' coaches typically seek out student athletes for admission to their programs.

To improve your chances of obtaining an athletic scholarship, build positive relationships with your current coaches as well as prospective schools' athletic departments. Many schools may not provide you a full academic ride, but they can still provide you a partial scholarship. This might pay for books, meal plan, housing, and/or tuition. Either way, anything helps!

Athletic scholarships can help you achieve a post-secondary education. However, they come at an expense. Athletic scholarships are contingent upon annual performance *and* maintaining Satisfactory Academic Progress (SAP).

Should you secure an athletic scholarship, there are many rules and regulations that you must follow. You can't decide to attend school but stop going to practice. In my tenure as a team manager and athletic administrator, I saw firsthand the loss of many students' scholarships because they forget the terms and conditions. As a student athlete, sports are your job. That "job" essentially pays for your college education. Therefore, you must make sure that you uphold your image and merit.

Ensuring that you adhere to your contract, NCAA rules and regulations, and the requirements of the compliance staff is imperative for *renewal*. This point is very important, as many students do not follow the rules and regulations surrounding their scholarship.

Sadly, some students just don't understand (or remember) the value of what they are receiving. They take advantage of the benefits and perks offered to them as an athlete. And by the time they remember the standards they agreed to uphold, it's too late.

College coaches are constantly on the lookout for prospects and new students eager to work hard. If you don't continue to show your coaches and the school that you're worth this opportunity, it can easily be taken away . . . without reconsideration.

Here's the good news. If you aren't selected for an athletic scholarship and are still passionate about playing at the collegiate level, you may be able to become a walk-on. You may be eligible to walk on the team and prove to the team and university that you're an asset for the athletics department.

Remaining optimistic is important. Students lose athletic scholarships daily, and the money is re-gifted to other students. Just know there is still a chance, but you will have to work for it!

Also keep this in mind: Every year athletic departments get new budgets that may allow them to provide you additional funds. However, depending on the physical state of the university, they can also revoke scholarships if it's no longer in their budget. Please be aware of the rules around an athletic scholarship prior committing to a school.

INTERNSHIPS

When I attended Howard University in D.C. my junior year, I received a Fox News scholarship and internship for $5000. I was given half prior to starting the internship and the remaining $2500 upon completing the internship. It also came with a transportation stipend that paid for my transportation to and from home.

It was an honor to be a broadcast journalism major working for one of the top broadcast news networks in the world. At the age of twenty, I was able to develop my craft and learn from the best of the best in the television industry. Additionally it helped my mom, who was laid off, to pay for my college tuition.

The scholarship money was sent directly to my student account. Many internships and scholarships will not give you the money directly. They will send it to the school to pay off your account balance.

I actually stumbled across this opportunity by visiting my school's advisory center, where I browsed folders of different scholarship and internship opportunities.

While in college, you should try and secure internship opportunities. This is a great way to network, gain professional experience in your career field, and potentially gain scholarships to help offset your educational expenses. Sometimes internships can lead to your first job after college.

DOES YOUR EMPLOYER OFFER TUITION BENEFITS?

While I worked various part-time jobs throughout college, many of them offered me tuition benefits. For example, as an outreach representative, I received a $1000 a semester (which was contingent upon receiving a C or better in my course).

This was money paid directly to me from my employer that I didn't have to pay back.

Before you apply for a new job, take the time to research the benefits the organization offers. Even after you graduate from college, you might want to go back to school for another degree but not take out loans. Finding jobs with great tuition benefits can minimize out-of-pocket expense and debt.

If you already have a job, ask around at your current job for any tuition benefits they may offer.

Employers have different terms and conditions, so before receiving those funds, thoroughly understand the rules and regulations around that money.

If you are working, you can also look into investment/savings accounts at your job.

Community Scholarships

Many local organizations offer scholarships to students. Find them by speaking with teachers and counselors. Nowadays, you can even raise your own money for college tuition through crowd funding sites such as Go Fund Me (https://www.gofundme.com/).

If you belong to a church, ask if there are any scholarship opportunities. My church, First Baptist Church of Lincoln Gardens in Somerset, New Jersey, had a great scholarship program for high school seniors. The church would hold events throughout the year, and all proceeds would go to the upcoming graduates. All you had to do was fill out paperwork, attend the meetings, and submit your official college documentation.

Also, many people within the church work for different organizations that provide scholarships to students. So, make connections with your church members and begin to ask around.

In addition, you can join local groups, such as beauty pageants, debutante balls, sorority/fraternity mentorship programs, and local charitable organizations, to find potential scholarship opportunities.

DISABILITY SCHOLARSHIPS

Disabilities that impact the way you learn can earn you an opportunity to continue your post-secondary education. Disability scholarships are available to students who have physical or mental disabilities.

Search on the Internet and ask at your prospective school for scholarships for students with disabilities.

For example, the District of Columbia Rehabilitation Services Administration (RSA) in Washington, D.C. provides employment opportunities and educational benefits for people with disabilities within the D.C. metropolitan area. In order to utilize the educational benefits, you must fill out an intake form and meet with an RSA counselor to develop an Individualized Educational Plan (IEP). Applicants must still apply for a FAFSA and may utilize their grants and loans if they like. Additionally, your prospective school has to provide RSA an invoice of your classes and book amounts, so the RSA can pay the school directly. This is a prime example of additional opportunities for students with disabilities.

For more information on RSA in your state, visit https://rsa.ed.gov/.

✓ Search on the Internet and ask at your prospective school for scholarships for students with disabilities.

VETERAN BENEFITS

There are many veteran benefits for:

- students who are dependents of veteran parents,
- spouses of veterans, and
- students who are veterans.

These benefits can help you complete your educational goals while minimizing debt.

Military benefits are not only for a traditional college degree. Under the GI Bill, you may seek a post-secondary education in any technical, graduate, or professional program. You can complete on-the-job training and apprenticeships (certificate training courses) if you choose not to attend a traditional college. You have up to fifteen years after active duty to utilize this program.

You can use your military benefits simultaneously with loans, scholarships, and grants. These benefits typically do not exceed thirty-six months of post-secondary education. Therefore it's imperative to plan the best way to utilize these benefits.

Post-9/11 GI Bill is a program to receive educational benefits, granted to any service member with ninety or more days of service on or after September 2001 and an honorable discharge. Benefits vary depending on how much time you spent in your perspective branch of the military. Therefore, you must contact the VA to determine the benefits you qualify for.

This bill typically pays for tuition, books, fees, and housing expenses for you, your spouse, or your children. The VA pays the school directly and provides a housing stipend directly to the student.

The amount of the stipend depends on whether you are attending online or ground classes. Students receive more of a housing stipend if they attend classes on college grounds.

If you choose to utilize these benefits or transfer them to your spouse or children, you must speak with a VA representative to review your Certificate of Eligibility (COE), which details your amount of benefits. If you attend a state/public school, all tuition and fees will be paid. However, if you attend a private or foreign school, up to $21,970.46 per academic year will be paid.

If your Cost of Attendance (COA) exceeds this amount, you may be eligible to receive benefits under the **Yellow Ribbon Program**.

The Yellow Ribbon Program provides additional funds to cover your educational expenses. However, only certain schools participate in this program, so it is imperative to research which schools participate.

Be sure to speak with your VA representative at your prospective school and the Veteran Administration to see if you are eligible for Yellow Ribbon benefits.

- "You must be eligible for the maximum benefit rate under the Post-9/11 GI Bill
- you must not be on active duty or a spouse using transferred entitlement
- your school must agree to participate in the Yellow Ribbon Program
- your school must have not offered Yellow Ribbon to more than the maximum number of individuals, as stated in their participation agreement
- your school must certify your enrollment to VA and provide Yellow Ribbon Program information" (http://www.benefits.va.gov/gibill/yellow_ribbon.asp)

"You may be eligible if you fit the following circumstances:

- you served an aggregate period of 36 months in active duty after September 10, 2001.
- you were honorably discharged from active duty for a service-connected disability and you served 30 continuous days after September 10, 2001.
- you are a dependent eligible for Transfer of Entitlement under the Post-9/11 GI Bill based on the service eligibility criteria listed above" (http://www.benefits.va.gov/gibill/yellow_ribbon.asp).

Dependent students and spouses can also utilize **Chapter 35**, or DEA. "**The Survivors' and Dependents' Educational Assistance (DEA) Program** offers education and training opportunities to eligible dependents of veterans who are permanently and totally disabled due to a service-related condition or of veterans who died while on active duty or as a result of a service-related condition" (http://www.benefits. va.gov/gibill/survivor_dependent_assistance.asp).

However, these benefits are not paid directly to the school but to the student. In order to qualify, you must speak with your financial aid office and your VA representative. Your family may be eligible for more than one VA educational benefit; if that is the case, you must elect which benefit to receive (http://www.benefits.va.gov/gibill/docs/pamphlets/ch35_pamphlet_2.pdf).

- ✓ For more information on military educational benefits, visit http://www.benefits.va.gov/gibill/handouts_ forms.asp. You will be able to review all benefits and scholarships the Veteran Administration offers.

Apply for Scholarships

The above opportunities are available, but you must be willing to do the research and execute all aspects of the application process.

Applying for scholarships can be a tedious task. You might start thinking you have better things to do than fill out scholarship applications all day. You don't! During your college search, there is no time to sleep! If you want to go to college and not be buried in debt, you must sacrifice now and do your research.

You're investing in your future. You might not see the importance of making the Herculean effort now, but you will be grateful in the long run.

Typically, scholarships are competitive, so you must be strategic and optimistic when applying. Don't get discouraged if you apply and do not hear back. Keep applying and stay motivated.

If you are awarded a scholarship, invest yourself in maintaining your GPA. You may be able to receive future funding based on your academic excellence.

Part 3
Navigating the Jungle
of Student Loans

5. Advantages and Options: Federal Student Loans

Student Loans

LOANS! The word every person loves to hate. "Student loans make up the nation's second-largest consumer debt market" (http://www.consumerfinance.gov/newsroom/cfpb-concerned-about-widespread-servicing-failures-reported-by-student-loan-borrowers/). According to Market Watch, "the outstanding balance of the nation's student loans is growing by an estimated $2,726.27 every second" (http://www.marketwatch.com/story/every-second-americans-get-buried-under-another-3055-in-student-loan-debt-2015-06-10).

Every student I've come across has asked, "Do I have to take out loans?" Fact is, loans can help you pay for your college education if you don't have sufficient means to pay for it upfront.

A student loan is self-help aid. It is money that you have to pay back.

In other words, if you take out any loan, you are responsible for paying it back.

Some students and parents try to transfer loans to one another. Yet once a loan is taken out by a person, it is their loan—they are responsible to pay it back. You cannot add anyone else on the loan or transfer the balance for someone else to pay off. Even if you file for bankruptcy, student loan debt will NEVER be removed!

And if you don't receive a degree, the harsh reality is that you'll be repaying money to the federal government or private lender for a degree you never received. "Many students leave school with onerous levels of student loan debt they must begin to repay almost right away—debt that can not only tax their ability to make ends meet as they embark on their careers, but also jeopardize their financial security far into the future" (http://research.prudential.com/documents/ rp/paying_for_college_a_practical_guide_for_families.pdf).

Therefore, consider your options carefully before applying for a loan. Also, be sure to read all the terms and conditions. Not all student loans are the same, so *make sure you do your research.*

Federal vs. Private Loans

It is always best to choose a federal loan before a private loan because of the benefits.

- Federal loans have fixed interests rates, where the rates never change throughout the life of the loan.
- The federal government also has the lowest interest rates and flexible repayment methods, whereas private lenders' interest rates tend to be higher and some may require you to begin paying immediately.

For federal loans, the interest rate varies depending on the loan type and (for most types of federal student loans) the first disbursement date of the loan. Federal law determines the interest rates for federal student loans.

The stipulation with federal loans is that as an undergrad you must maintain over a 2.0 GPA every semester/quarter in order to receive aid. In contrast, most private loans aren't disbursed according to your academic performance.

To sum up:

Federal Loans	Private Loans
funded by the federal government	funded by banks
repayment begins six months after you graduate, leave school, or change your enrollment status to less than half-time	many private student loans require payments while you are still in school
interest rate is fixed and is often lower than private loans	have variable interest rates, some greater than 18 percent
for most federal loans, a credit check is not required (except for PLUS Loans—details coming up shortly)	are credit based, so you may need an established credit record in order to secure a loan or a co-signer
offer deferment and/or forbearance options	private lenders may not offer deferment or forbearance options

While working at a post-secondary institution, I met a gentleman who had a $20,000 private student loan at a 12.99 percent interest rate. If he would have taken out his federal loans he would have saved 9.23%, as the federal interest rate for loans disbursed on or after 7/1/16 and before 7/1/17 was 3.76% for subsidized and unsubsidized loans. However, he was so desperate to finish school that he was willing to take out anything to accomplish his dreams.

That should serve as a reminder: Private loans should be your last choice when securing your education. A lot of private lenders defer your loan until after graduation or after you leave school. But they are not as forgiving with repayments like the federal government is.

Federal Loans: The Direct Loan Program

The U.S. Department of Education offers low interest loans at fixed interest rates directly to students and parents (thus, "direct loans") through the Federal Direct Loan Program. In other words, the Federal Direct Loan Program allows the student or parents to borrow *directly* from the government. Currently, the federal student loan debt is 1.3 trillion dollars!

Eligibility for this program is based on the information provided from the FAFSA. The aid provided by the government will be determined by your dependency status.

The Federal Direct Loan Program offers student loans that have fixed interests rates, where repayment begins six months after the student leaves school, drops below half-time, or graduates.

Loans within this program have annual limits that are based on grade level, Expected Family Contribution, and dependency status. The aggregate loan limit for a dependent student is $34,500, whereas an independent student can receive $57,500. Yet, some schools may cost $30K or more annually to attend. Therefore, you must be sure you are continuously finding external resources to fund your education.

There are two types of direct loans—subsidized and unsubsidized loans. The **subsidized loan** is based on financial need, where interest (as well as payment) begins six months after the student leaves school, drops below half-time, or graduates. The **unsubsidized loan** is non-need based, where interest accrues once the loan is disbursed and during all grace periods. A grace period is the six months after you leave school or drop below full-time; after six months the loan servicer requests payment.

"Subsidized and unsubsidized loans are federal student loans for eligible students to help cover the cost of higher education at a four-year college or university, community college, or trade, career, or technical school. The U.S. Department of Education offers eligible students at participating schools Direct Subsidized Loans and Direct Unsubsidized Loans. (Some people refer to these loans as Stafford Loans or Direct Stafford Loans.)" (https://studentaid. ed.gov/sa/types/loans/subsidized-unsubsidized)

Federal Direct Loans Eligibility

	Dependent	Independent
Freshman	$5,500 ($3,500 sub / $2,000 unsub)	$9,500 ($3,500 sub / $6,000 unsub)
Sophomore	$6,500 ($4,500 sub / $2,000 unsub)	$10,500 ($4,500 sub / $6,000 unsub)
Third Year & Beyond	$7,500 ($5,500 sub / $2,000 unsub)	$12,500 ($5,500 sub / $7,000 unsub)
Aggregate Limits:	**$31,000**	**$57,500**

As you can see, dependency status has a notable effect on the amount of direct loans the federal government will provide. If you are determined dependent, you will get less funding. If you are independent, you will receive more funding. However, for both independent and dependent status, you may not exceed $23,000 in subsidized loans. Therefore, it is important for you to understand the effects of dependency status on your prospective financial aid award package.

Subsidized or Unsubsidized Loan?

If a student is offered a subsidized loan, he or she should accept it instead of an unsubsidized loan, because the government pays interest on the subsidized while the student is enrolled full-time and during the grace period.

Subsidized	Unsubsidized
for undergraduate students who have financial need	for undergraduate students who don't have financial need
the college determines the amount of your loan, which cannot go beyond your financial need	the college determines the amount of your loan, based on your Cost of Attendance and your other financial aid
"The U.S. Department of Education pays the interest on a Direct Subsidized Loan: ■ while you're in school at least half-time ■ the first six months after you leave school (referred to as a grace period*) ■ if you're eligible for a deferment" (https://studentaid.ed.gov /sa/types/loans/subsidized-unsubsidized).	"Interest begins on a Direct Unsubsidized Loan as soon as the loan is disbursed and accrues during all periods. If you select to pay the interest while you are in school and during all periods, you may lower your overall principal balance" (https://studentaid.ed.gov /sa/types/loans/subsidized-unsubsidized).

Federal Loans: Direct PLUS Loan

As explained by https://studentaid.ed.gov/sa/types/ loans/plus, "PLUS Loans are federal loans that graduate or professional degree students and parents of dependent undergraduate students can use to help pay education expenses. The U.S. Department of Education makes Direct PLUS Loans to eligible borrowers through schools participating in the Direct Loan Program.

"Here's a quick overview of Direct PLUS Loans:

- The U.S. Department of Education is the lender.
- The borrower must not have an adverse credit history.
- The maximum loan amount is the student's Cost of Attendance (determined by the school) minus any other financial aid received."
- If you have an adverse credit history, you may still receive a Direct PLUS Loan by obtaining an endorser.
- Also, "if a parent borrower is unable to secure a PLUS Loan, the undergraduate dependent student may be eligible for additional unsubsidized loans" (https://studentaid.ed.gov/sa/types/loans/plus# eligibility).

In order to be eligible, you must complete a FAFSA.

Direct PLUS Loans: Parent PLUS/Grad PLUS

You may apply for a Parent/Grad PLUS Loan by visiting https://studentloans.gov/myDirectLoan/index.action. They have no aggregate limit, yet the limit cannot exceed the student's Cost of Attendance.

As a parent, your repayments typically begin 60 days after the loan disburses, yet if your child is enrolled, you can defer to pay once your student leaves school. Also, you may be able to qualify for the grace period as well.

If you get denied for a Parent PLUS Loan, your child's dependent loan limit will increase to the independent loan limit amounts.

It is understandable that not all parents are able to secure a PLUS Loan alone, due to their credit history. Yet you may be able to find a cosigner to endorse the loan for you. Student, let's say your mother can't secure a PLUS Loan. You can ask anyone, such as your grandmother, aunt, brother, cousin, and so on, to endorse the loan.

Note: If the borrower fails to pay the PLUS Loan once it goes into repayment, the lender (the government) will seek the endorser. Both you and they will be tied to the loan until it is completely paid off. Be sure to explain this to anyone who is trying to endorse.

Also note: Once a parent and/or guardian secures a parent PLUS Loan, the loan (the debt) cannot be transferred to the child (college student) to repay. If a parent takes out a PLUS Loan for the child's education, the parent is solely responsible for repayment.

I have heard many stories of parents making their children pay off their monthly PLUS Loan payments. Student, there is no law against that; it's simply an agreement between you and your parent. But keep in mind that if *you* borrowed student loans plus you're helping your parent repay the loans *they* took out for you, you will be paying *a lot* of money each month immediately after graduation.

FEES

When you take out any federal loan, an origination fee will be assessed. So if you take out $5,500 in sub/unsub loans, your origination fee will be 1.068 percent (current percentage; subject to change). Meaning by the time you get the funds, that amount will not be $5,500, but $5,441.

Therefore, you must financially plan and understand what the exact amount of the loan will be, including interest.

Also, fees may be assessed monthly if you fail to pay on time.

Repayment Estimator Calculator

The repayment estimator calculator located at https://studentloans.gov/myDirectLoan/mobile/repayment/repaymentEstimator.action is a great tool to estimate your potential repayments postgraduation. It will allow you to see the total costs of securing a college education and see what your potential expenses can be.

These estimates will show exactly how much debt you may be in if you do not continue to seek external resources such as grants and scholarships. It will also show you the total interest on the loan you may be paying over time.

✓ Making payments on loans while in school will help you save in the future. Log on to https://myfedloan.org/ to see the interest savings calculator.

Terms, Conditions, Payments

Before accepting, review your Federal Direct Loan's terms and conditions on https://studentloans.gov/myDirectLoan/

index.action so you to understand the terms and conditions of the loan prior to it being disbursed.

In order for federal loans to disburse, you must complete the Entrance Counseling and Master Promissory Note (MPN). These two items are critical because the government wants to counsel you on these loans, repayment methods, and receive your contact information to ensure you will pay these loans back. (Parents must do entrance counseling and MPN as well if they are borrowing a PLUS.)

Additionally, once you graduate or drop below half-time, they will make you complete an Exit Counseling, which prepares you for repaying your federal student loans.

It is in your best interest to pay back your federal loan in a short time frame, so you won't have to pay extra years of interest. Paying more than the monthly amount due will put more value to the principle of the loan.

Note: Federal loans do not increase annually as the cost of tuition rises, which may make it harder to pay off your bill if you don't have other resources.

 ✓ Track your federal student loan history through the National Student Loan Data System (NSLDS) at https://www.nslds.ed.gov/nslds/nslds_SA/. The system will also show you your loan history, disbursements, grant history, and your federal loan servicers contact info.

6. Still More Possibilities: Private Student Loans

If you exhaust all your resources (grants, scholarships, federal loans) and you still have a balance, you may need to secure a private loan for the balance. However, securing a private loan may be difficult since they are based on creditworthiness. Most students (97 percent) need a cosigner in order to secure a private loan.

"Parents and grandparents put their financial futures on the line by co-signing private student loans to help family members achieve the dream of higher education," says Consumer Financial Protection Bureau director Richard Cordray (http://www.consumerfinance.gov/about-us/newsroom/cfpb-finds-90-percent-of-private-student-loan-borrowers-who-applied-for-co-signer-release-were-rejected/).

You can't receive a private loan by completing the FAFSA. In order to secure a private loan, you'll need to contact your bank, credit union, loan servicer, or a similar resource that provides student loans.

Before Taking Out a Private Loan

It is wise to speak with a college financial aid administrator before taking out a private loan to see exactly how much money you will need.

Forecasting your expenses can help you in the long run. Reviewing the Cost of Attendance, scholarships, grants, and loans will allow you to see what your out-of-pocket expenses and repayment methods can be. As the cost of college increases, so do debt and interest rates. Using the repayment estimator calculator will give you a better sense of what your projected expenses will be over the next few years.

Next, do the research on different lenders, because everyone has different interest rates.

How long does it take to secure a private loan? Typically, private loans have a turnaround time of fifteen business days from the date the person applies. The approval is sent to the school, and the school has to verify if there is room in the budget to accept the amount.

However, if approved for the loan, you have a ten-day processing period called *the right to cancel* period if you do not want the loan anymore.

Note: With private loans, there is no leeway regarding repayment. Some private lenders may make you start paying as soon as the loan is given to you.

Following is the loan comparison table, duplicated from the previous chapter. Consider carefully the challenges that come with private loans.

Federal Loans	Private Loans
funded by the federal government	funded by banks
repayment begins six months after you graduate, leave school, or change enrollment status to less than half-time	some private student loans require payments while you are still in school
interest rate is fixed and is often lower than private loans	have variable interest rates, some greater than 18 percent
for most federal loans, a credit check is not required (except for PLUS Loans—details coming up shortly)	are credit based, so you may need an established credit record in order to secure a loan or a co-signer
offer deferment and/or forbearance options	private lenders may not offer deferment or forbearance options

Of key importance are the less flexible repayment options. Borrowers must understand that if they borrow private loans and fall into a financial situation where they aren't able to keep up payments, there may not be forbearance or deferment options, as many private lenders do not offer these options.

In 2014, the Consumer Finance Bureau did a research study that investigated 5,300 complaints from private student lenders. The study suggests that "a number of borrowers are eager to protect their credit and avoid the consequences of delinquency and default. When these borrowers anticipated that they would be unable to pay, often due to difficulties securing adequate employment, they sought options for a reduced payment plan. But many of these consumers received responses from lenders and servicers that they were unwilling to offer an alternative repayment option for their loans" (http://files.consumerfinance. gov/f/201410_cfpb_report_annual-report-of-the-student-loan-ombudsman.pdf).

Before signing, make sure you have exhausted all of your resources and, as I said above, shop around to view *all* your options. Some private lenders have initiated programs to assist the lender in repayment, though, as you might expect, very few lenders have implemented this policy.

7. Putting It All Together

Smart Borrowing

Did you know that the national student debt is $1.3 trillion dollars? Americans owe more in student loan debt than credit card debt (http://www.politifact.com/virginia/statements/2014/jun/10/ mark-warner/warner-says-us-student-debt-has-surpassed-credit-c/). Excessive student loan debt is affecting people of all ages, as this has become a multigenerational issue.

Students are impacted since financial burdens interfere with success in the classroom and reduce the chance of program completion and job opportunities. Therefore it is essential to fund your education wisely by borrowing what you need—and *only* what you need.

Borrowing does not have to be a burden if you borrow smart. You don't have to take out all the loans the school approves you for, and you may alter the loan amount by filling out an award adjustment request form. If you only need $5,000 to pay off your balance, why borrow $10K, $15K, or $20K? When people borrow more than they need, that generates a refund. The refund comes from an account balance having an excess of funds once the account is paid.

Sometimes you can receive a refund because you have excess funds. Do not immediately blow it on materialistic things, but save it! You never know when you're going to be in a situation where you need it. I can't tell you how many situations I was in during college where I didn't have any additional money to help me out. Thankfully, I had the option of calling Mom and Dad, but not everyone has that option.

Borrow what you need and not what you want. Remember, this is money that YOU are going to have to repay. As my colleague Crawley would say, we may want a red Lamborghini, but that does not mean we can afford one. Therefore, be smart with your borrowing.

Parents, if you take out a loan and there is an excess of funds once the student account is paid, a refund will be generated. Therefore, save this money! You might not be approved to receive a loan next year, so use what you save to continue funding your child's education.

Parents are just as guilty as the student with blowing refunds on things not related to their children's education. These loans can potentially affect your retirement and personal goals. Therefore, parents too should be borrowing smart!

Smart Communication

Don't get an attitude with your prospective school's financial aid office. I learned this lesson myself: You never know who you are talking to.

When your phone call is being transferred to financial aid, you never know who might pick up. So be polite, honest, and charismatic. That will get you a long way.

You want to build a positive relationship with everyone you talk to in the office. These are the people who will (or won't) help you to find additional funds and future opportunities.

You don't want to be the student or parent that every professional hates to speak to. Ensure that when you speak with financial aid you have all your questions ready to ask.

Also, write down the names of EVERYONE you speak to. I have heard and dealt with many situations in my tenure as a financial aid administrator. Students may say So and So said xyz, yet they do not remember the name of So and So, therefore no verifiable proof exists regarding what was actually said.

When dealing with your money and education, be sure to write names and what exactly was communicated, and follow up with those professionals when needed.

FERPA

In an effort to protect your records, parents are not able to call on your behalf without a FERPA form on file. FERPA, which is the Family Educational Rights and Privacy Act, is a federal law that protects the privacy of student records.

Therefore, students must sign a FERPA form in order to allow their parents/guardians access to their records. If this form is not on file, parents cannot gain access to student records, which includes grades, courses, and student account information, even though they may be the one paying the tuition.

Parents, if you would like to call the financial aid office on behalf of your child, please ensure that your child signs off to authorize you to gain access to their account.

Compare and Contrast Financial Aid Award Offers

Try to negotiate your financial aid award. As a financial aid professional, I understand that the college financial aid process can be cumbersome. Yet you must work together with your family to get through the process, and have patience to see it through. ·

Once students receive their award packages from the financial aid office, some are unhappy with the awards granted to them. Some may feel that it's not a true reflection of their family and that they need more money. If you aren't satisfied with your award letter, you may be able to negotiate.

I encourage students in this situation to speak with the financial aid administrators and see if they may be eligible for additional funding. "I appreciate all you've done and I want to attend school here, but what you gave me is not enough to get me through the semester/years. Do you have any more funds I can qualify for?" You might be in luck and get additional funds. You never know when financial aid has extra funds to give out.

Comparing and contrasting financial aid offers is a must. Depending on your financial situation, it can make or break your final decision. If one school isn't offering you anything but others are, then go where the money is. Remember, you do not want to be buried in thousands of dollars of debt postgraduation.

Will Tuition and Cost of Attendance Increase over Time?

Affordability will be the most important thing when trying to finish your studies. It may be affordable in the beginning, but it might not be over the long term.

Education expenses can increase throughout your tenure. New fees and prices may be added to your student account as the college gains new programs, staff, and services.

Keep in mind that the cost of living in some states has gotten higher and higher. That means the school and everything around it may also cost more and more each year.

Ask each prospective school if tuition will increase over time. Please review their tuition prices over the last few years to see if there has been an increase. If tuition has an annual increase, you'll want to ask yourself if you can afford the increases.

The specific program you choose may impact your tuition rate as well. For example, biology majors may incur lab fees, material fees, and higher book costs.

As a broadcast journalism major, I had additional costs depending on which course I took. All were mandatory toward my degree since I needed equipment that would allow me to execute projects. Having to get the software, computers, production classes, and cameras added to my Cost of Attendance.

Sometimes you get less for your money from universities, due to the fact that employees and resources can be stripped from schools' budgets, even though Cost of Attendance increases. Be sure to check out the prospective school's Cost of Attendance over the past few years.

Finally, remember that going to school requires money to do things. Don't get me wrong—there are a lot of free things to do. Yet, as a college student, you may want to go out to eat with friends, attend events, and pay for transportation. Therefore, be sure to pick a school where its location is affordable for you.

Consider these factors as you compare and contrast your financial aid offers.

Is the Award Renewable and Guaranteed Annually?

Many schools will provide you financial aid offers your first year only. Check to see if the scholarships they are offering are renewable. Who wants to go to school one year with a scholarship, but not receive it the following years? I've come across plenty of students who have received $20,000 to $30,000 scholarships for the first year but nothing for the years after. Now they're stuck at an institution they can't pay for and are taking out private loans to try to stay afloat. Or some have actually been kicked out of school.

Many renewable awards may come with stipulations. Some awards can be GPA based or based on financial need.

Following up with the financial aid office before accepting your offer is crucial. It will allow you to understand and financially plan for your program.

Weigh all of the above considerations carefully before accepting a college's financial aid offer.

Accept Your Offer

After reviewing all of your admissions and financial aid packages, you must accept your financial aid offer. Offers can be accepted electronically, by mail, or by fax, and you must accept your package by the deadline your prospective school gives you. Some schools may offer you more aid, but if you do not accept it by the deadline, you could potentially lose it. So don't wait too long to make your decisions.

Maintain the focus!

Don't stop dreaming and striving for excellence. Even while you are in school, continue to research offers that will provide assistance, financially and otherwise. The connections you make throughout your college career may help you in the years to come.

8. Pay over Time with a Payment Plan

Depending on your family situation and the school you attend, you may be able to sign up for a payment plan. If you don't have all the money up front, a payment plan will allow you to pay off the balance over time (i.e., term/semester) and most plans will not accrue interest.

Many schools offer this flexible payment option. This allows you to stay enrolled in classes throughout the semester.

However, if you miss a payment with the school, there could be consequences (i.e. dropped classes, fee, etc.).

Some schools may make you sign up for a payment plan prior to enrolling. Therefore, follow up with your prospective school's student accounts department to gain more insight into the payment options available.

Even with a payment option, you must make sure you allocate enough money each month to pay off your plan. Many of these plans compel you to automatically link a checking, savings, or credit card account once you enroll, for automatic monthly deduction.

Be certain there are funds in that account for payment on the due date. If there are no funds, the school may charge you a penalty for being delinquent.

Read all the terms and conditions for a payment plan prior to enrolling. There may be a minimal fee to sign up for a payment plan.

Overall, this flexible option is definitely a great way to pay your college bill.

Importance of Not Rolling Over Debt into Future Terms

In my tenure as a financial aid professional, I have seen many students sign up for payment plans just to stay enrolled. Unfortunately, they are often unable to afford the payments though they believe they'll have the money by the end of the term/semester. Many of them do not pay off the balance, which then rolls into the next term/semester.

As I pointed out above, many schools will drop your classes because of nonpayment. Once delinquent on a payment plan, schools may require you to sign up for a past-due payment plan and put down a certain percentage of the balance.

When signing up for the payment plan, be sure to pick one that will work for your financial situation. Sometimes you may not want to sit out a semester, yet if it is not financial feasible, then you must make that hard decision.

Here's a story.

One day I was walking to another office to drop off documents, and I met this student and his mentor. It just so happens that the student was inquiring how to get back into school. I asked him to describe his situation to see how I might offer him resources.

He explained to me that he owed more than $40,000 for the prior year. Since he hadn't maintained Satisfactory Academic Progress (SAP)—above a 2.0 GPA—he was ineligible to receive his financial aid award package.

Since his loans did not pay out, he had signed up for a payment plan, yet he was not in a financial situation to make payments. As a result, the university didn't allow him to enroll another year until he paid off the debt.

Having $40,000 in debt at twenty years old with no means to pay for it is very challenging. He couldn't even transfer to another school if he wanted to because the registrar's office will not release transcript unless all balances are paid.

How does the story end? After twelve months of trying to find a solution, the student advocated and received tons of donor support that allowed him to return to his studies. Unfortunately this happy ending does not happen to everyone. There are many students with balances just as high if not higher who cannot get back into school.

Students with prior balances typically apply to private lenders to secure a loan to pay it off. However, the interest rates aren't fixed and monthly payments may start immediately.

Some scholarships may assist with paying off prior balances, but you must research to find them.

Understanding the Fine Print

Many scholarships, grants, and loans have terms and conditions. Credit and loan companies prey on young individuals. When signing any financial aid document, you must make sure you fully understand the fine print.

Financial aid documents can become overwhelming, especially after filling out tons of scholarship and admissions applications. Yet you must make sure you read and approve of everything before signing off.

Everything may sound good for the current time, but you have to keep the future in mind. Live each day for tomorrow.

Ensuring that you grow your wealth and make smart decisions is paramount when signing your name on the dotted line.

Part 4
Making the Most
of Your College Years

9. Working through College

Your Primary College Goal: Academic Excellence

Working during your college years has abundant benefits. It will help offset your educational expenses, help your bank account, and provide you with professional experience.

However, it also can get in the way of your studies. Some students begin to concentrate more on making money and tend to forget their responsibilities as a student. Staying on top of your studies is important for academic excellence and potential opportunities. It is very easy to become lazy in your studies because you're working. Trust me—I've been there!

As a full-time student and part-time employee, you must wisely manage your time.

Maintaining academic excellence throughout your college career is your primary goal. It's your reason for being in college! You are paying top dollar for an education, so learn all you can. Do not let your dollars go to waste.

Who wants to stay longer than needed because their grades haven't maintained Satisfactory Academic Progress (SAP)? The longer you stay in school, the more debt you may acquire.

I've met many students who exceeded their undergraduate aggregate loan limit of $57,500 and still did not receive any type of degree. By the time they got serious about their studies, there were no more federal loans left.

Every withdrawal, dropped class, and F affects your completion rate and GPA. Be smart before failing and withdrawing.

Academic excellence, on the other hand, can lead to potential opportunities. For example, the GPA from your freshman year can impact your eligibility for the next year. In other words, maintaining stellar grades allows you to be eligible for institutional resources that you may not have been eligible for a year prior.

Starting off strong will put you in a good position.

At the end of my freshman year, my GPA was 3.6. This allowed me to get donor scholarships and funds from my department and external resources, even though my parents were not financially needy. It also gave me leverage for future years. If I ever received a bad grade, my GPA would not be not drastically affected.

Your high GPA can make you eligible for additional scholarships or internships. Institutional resources are given annually to students who meet certain criteria set by a department or the financial aid office.

New scholarships (donor scholarships, merit scholarships, department scholarships) and grants are developed annually. Therefore, you want to make sure that whenever they are available you are able to be eligible to qualify for those funds because of your GPA.

Many students who do not have professional experience can use their GPAs to navigate and secure potential opportunities, such as a great career upon graduation.

Making the Most of a Job Opportunity

Now that the importance of academic excellence is solidified in your mind, you can now consider employment.

Throughout your academic career you should continue to search for external resources to help develop your professional experience. Working through school gives you an advantage. After you graduate, many employers want to see that you were actively working while in school. This could be through work-study, part-time employment, or internships. These external resources are beneficial and will contribute to your student account.

Here is another consideration. After college graduation, do you plan to attend graduate school? Many students do not want to pursue graduate studies due to the debt they have acquired throughout their undergrad years. Other students do, though some graduate programs are difficult to get into, depending on your undergrad GPA and the program you are trying to get admitted to. Graduate programs want to see that you will be an asset to their program. Therefore, it is imperative to secure some form of an internship or employment throughout your undergraduate studies.

As I stated earlier in the book, many employers will pay for you to go to school to seek a degree within the field of your choice or a field tailored to the career you are in.

This is an added potential benefit of working throughout college: For decades, companies have seen the stress on employees who try to pay off their student debt. Recently companies have begun to offer to help them pay off student loan debt. So far, only 3 percent of companies offer this amazing benefit.

However, the number will continue to grow since many companies are coming on board with this incentive.

For instance, investment company Fidelity "will put $2,000 a year toward student loan repayments for employees who have worked at the company for at least six months, up to a total of $10,000" (http://www.bloomberg.com/news/articles/2016-03-15/etsy-and-fidelity-expand-their-family-leave-policies).

As a result, employees can start to save up for retirement and keep more of their earnings through work. Therefore, look for employers who will assist you to pay off your student loan debt.

Make the most of a job opportunity. When applying for a job, make sure you pick the right hours. Overnight shifts followed by classes in the morning can be very stressful. Most traditional college classes are between 9:00 a.m. and 5:00 p.m., so establish a schedule that allows sufficient time for classes, homework, and your job.

Working during college can definitely help build your time management skills.

By my junior year of college, working allowed me to become more financially independent. I secured my own apartment and then maintained my monthly living expenses. Moving off campus saved my parents more money because on-campus fees—room and board (meals)—dropped away.

If you move off campus, you too will have to pay your expenses every month.

Also, the earnings you make in college as a single (unmarried) tax filer must be reported if it is over $10,150. A parent can claim their child on their taxes if the child made less than $10,150. If not, the child must file their own taxes and add it to their FAFSA information. This could impact your financial aid package if added to your and your family's household income.

While attending Howard University going into my junior year, I obtained a job at PNC Bank as well as an internship with Fox News Channel headquarters in Washington, D.C. The job allowed me to pay my monthly and personal expenses, and the internship paid my student account. These two opportunities helped me so that my parents could focus on my tuition.

Having the ability to work while you are in school can be very rewarding! If you do well in your work or internship, your employer may be able to offer you a permanent position postgraduation.

10. Budgeting: Short-term Status versus Long-term Success

Students do not want to move back home immediately after graduation. Yet, if you don't financially plan and actively seek career opportunities, then the only option is to return home until you can get on your feet.

College allows you at least four years to get on your feet. Following are strategies to enable you to make that happen.

Plan Your Budget

Budget—another word everybody loves to hate! Why? Because no one wants to limit their spending. Yet money management is critical to your financial security.

To quote Dave Ramsey, "Creating a budget means telling your money where to go instead of wondering where your money went."

When budgeting, you want your expenses to be less than your income.

In order to make a budget, look at all your sources of income. The estimated amounts from your sources will determine how you can afford your fixed expenses such as rent, food, and tuition. Once those expenses are paid, you can determine how much you need to save and how much you are able to spend.

Subtract your fixed expenses from your total income to find out what income is disposable. For example, $2000 per month income, minus $1600 per month fixed expenses, equals $400 disposable income.

Live Within Your Means

Miscellaneous expenses may vary, and can quickly consume your disposable income. Miscellaneous expenses may include clothes, shoes, events, and more. Every haircut, pair of shoes purchased, and extracurricular activity expense should be monitored.

While attending Howard University, I saw on a daily basis students living above their means. College can be very intimidating. I was going to school with CEOs' daughters, pastors' sons, and celebrities' kids. Seeing them with Louis Vuitton bags, the best hair, and Christian Louboutin shoes made me feel like I was an outcast. I began paying $90 to $100 at the nail salon every two weeks. I took advantage of the financial security my parents gave me and constantly spent money. I had no money management skills or a budget set. Finally realizing that I spent $2,400 a year just at the nail salon was mind-boggling. In four years in college, I spent at least $9,600 on my nails that I wish I had now.

The issue here is our culture of advertising labels and brands—clever marketing tactics to coax money out of people. Trust me—I have been to hell and back over this! I am still learning to live within my means. It is tough!

Yes, you want your own apartment, car, new shoes, and the best phone money can buy. Yet, realistically, you can't afford it. Especially being a college student.

Wanting to feel as financially affluent as other students seem can cause you to do unnecessary things with your refund and savings accounts. Do not succumb to your environment.

Be you! You never know when you might need those additional funds that you are tempted to spend on materialistic items.

No matter who you are or what your parents/spouse may do, everyone needs to set some form of a budget and adjust their lifestyle to adhere to that. You must understand that it is only for a short time and you will be able to make more money soon.

I had to say to myself that I didn't have these things before college, so I will do just fine. Therefore, I didn't need them. To this day, I still do not own a $1,200 Louis Vuitton bag, because I would rather pay my rent than show off a bag just to appear as though I have high economic status.

Dr. Soaries says, "Sacrificing for our financial freedom is an ongoing process." Be sure to immerse yourself in your studies much more than the social aspects around you. Materialistic items are not going to help you excel in the classroom. Yet cultural pressures can cause you to spend unnecessary money. At the end of the day, you are in college to learn, not to prove to others that you have swag! As much effort as you put into trying to fit in, you should put the same effort into the classroom.

During college, live within your means. These years will establish the habits of how you manage your money for years to come. You may also inspire others around you to do the same.

Smart Shopping

When on a budget, it is important to shop smart. You can save in different ways by setting a schedule for your haircuts or not going out so much. Every time you swipe your card at 7-

Eleven® for soda and chips, that's $4 less than what you had. For the same amount you can stop at the grocery store and buy a larger quantity that will last longer.

Food can become very expensive. Read weekly store advertising to save a little money when shopping. Over time that adds up.

When going to Walmart, stick to what you came there for. Sometimes when we go into stores we begin to pick up everything we think we need when we actually don't. Those extra items can quickly reduce your disposable income.

Avoiding Credit Card Debt

The purpose of a credit card is to help you build good credit. Unfortunately, many college students acquire credit card debt.

Be sure you do not use credit card funds to buy things that you cannot afford upfront. If it is something you cannot afford on debit, do not buy it on credit! Instead, make minimal purchases that you know you can pay back.

Also, you want to make sure you make *more than* your minimum payment each month.

Remember, your credit history is vital to you securing life's luxuries, so be smart when using a credit card. Know your credit and debit card balances by monitoring your spending.

Little things add up. Online bank systems are now equipped to show you how much money you spent per category online. This will help you actually see how much you spend on specific items. Be sure to setup your bank account to begin to measure your expenses.

Build Your Bank Account Balance

Saving money in college is one of the best decisions you can make. As I look back on my prior experiences, I had so many opportunities to save money, yet I kept buying clothes (to go with the salon nails) so I could keep up with the latest fashion trends.

You do not know what life will be like postgraduation. Who knows if you will actually secure that dream job immediately after graduation? In many cases you will not, and if you do, you will likely not be making what you thought you would, at least to start out.

Making sure you will have financial security postgraduation is imperative. Knowing what you owe and borrowing smart can avoid unmanageable debt.

✓ Build your bank account balance as you work during your college years to save for the future.

The Decisions You Make

In college it is important to develop good decision-making skills, in financial and all other matters. If not, you will develop problems. Decisions can affect your everyday life. Ensuring that each decision will help your future is imperative to success!

No one is perfect and we all will make bad decisions along the way. Learn from yours. Discovering how to make good decisions through your college career will put you in a great position postgraduation.

These habits that you gain in college will last you throughout your lifetime.

Part 5
After Graduation: Funding Your Future

11. The Big Payoff of Your College Debt

Build a Good Relationship with Your Loan Servicer

If you secured a federal student loan, the U.S. Department of Education assigned your loan to a company. This company is known as a federal loan servicer. Soon after you graduate or drop below full time, the federal loan servicer will begin to seek repayment.

If you secured more than one federal loan, you may have more than one loan servicer.

Time is flying, so the six-month grace period can go by very quickly. Therefore it is critical to your financial security to create a repayment plan and build a relationship with your loan servicer. You may do this by contacting your federal loan servicer to speak to them about repayment options.

Become familiar with National Student Loan Data System (NSLDS) at https://www.nslds.ed.gov. This is a great tool to see your current loan and who your federal loan servicer is.

Note that it is important to update your personal information with the federal loan servicer if you relocate or change your telephone number. Report any change of your information immediately.

Avoid Default

When repaying your loans, you want to avoid becoming delinquent (missing a payment). I understand this may be difficult due to expenses postcollege. Some students do not even secure jobs postgraduation that will allow them to pay off student loans. It is difficult to maintain your cost of living and your loan repayments if you are barely making ends meet. If you don't have a job already, or one that enables you to support yourself and repay your loans, be sure to secure one immediately after graduation.

If you fail to make a payment on your federal student loan in 9 months or 270 days, your loan will begin to default. Across the country, default rates are rising due to cost-of-living expenses and unemployment rates. Betsy Mayotte with U.S. News & World Report provides a great example. "Let's say you defaulted on your $25,000 federal loan after a year. This example loan has a 5 percent interest rate, so right away your loan holder will add $1,250 to the balance in capitalized interest, plus any late fee amounts they may have charged you along the way. Now add the 24 percent collection cost of $6,300, and your $25,000 balance has grown to $32,800 in a year" (http://www.usnews.com/education/blogs/student-loan-ranger/2015/03/04/understand-the-consequences-of-student-loan-default).

Once you are in default, the Treasury Offset Program can seek your tax refund from the IRS until your debt is paid off. Legally they can garnish 15 percent of your wages from your paycheck if you fail to pay. In a worst-case scenario, they can sue you for the money.

Even worse long term, defaulting on any loan can have a negative effect on your credit score. That can affect your chances of securing employment, a house, car, and more.

Filing for bankruptcy will never eliminate your student loan debt.

Therefore you must avoid default, and you must never run from or avoid the loan servicer. If you have any difficulty repaying your loans, notify your loan servicer immediately. You do not want the loan servicer to begin to contact you.

When you notify your loan servicer of difficulty repaying, see if you can arrange a flexible payment option. The loan servicer may offer you a deferment (postponement for a given period of time) or forbearance (your monthly payments are temporarily reduced). These two options allow you additional time to repay the loan. However, during these periods, interest will still accrue on the unsubsidized loan.

If you have a *private* loan that has exceeded your time period of forbearance, you may see if the lender has a flexible payment option. Generally, most private student lenders do not offer additional in-school forbearance if the student requires additional time to obtain a degree or if the student returns to school to obtain a graduate degree. Some students complain that they are unable to begin making payments while enrolled in school and request additional forbearance in order to complete their programs of study. As a result, many of these students have reported that they were sent to collections or defaulted before graduating from school.

A federal loan servicer can also see if you may be eligible for loan forgiveness. There are two types of federal student loan forgiveness programs: Teacher Loan Forgiveness and Public Service Loan Forgiveness.

Teacher Loan Forgiveness: "If you teach full time for five complete and consecutive academic years in certain elementary and secondary schools or educational service agencies that serve low-income families, and meet other qualifications, you may be eligible for forgiveness of up to a combined total of $17,500 on certain federal student loans" (http://blog.ed.gov/2014/05/student-loan-forgiveness-and-other-ways-the-govern ment-can-help-you-repay-your-loans/).

The **Public Service Loan Forgiveness** (PSLF) **Program** is provided to federal borrowers who obtain employment within the public service industry. However, it is important to speak with your federal loan servicer to see if your career aligns with this program. If eligible, this program will forgive your remaining balance, yet you must make 120 on-time payments for 10 years in order to be considered for loan forgiveness. Follow up with your loan servicer to see if this is something you can take advantage of.

Remember, the more you delay paying off your student loan, the more interest will accrue. If you have more than one student loan, always pay off the loan with the highest interest rate first.

Loan Consolidation and Refinancing

You must always be aware of where you stand and the options available to you. If you have more than one student loan, you may be able to **consolidate** them into one. Consolidating your loans into one can help you keep track of all your student loan debt and make loan repayment more manageable.

How do you do this? Once you leave school or drop below full time, you may see that you have multiple loan servicers, as noted above. You can look into consolidating your federal loans by contacting your loan servicer. Again, you can find your loan servicer by logging onto the National Student Loan Data System (NSLDS) at https://www.nslds.ed.gov. You can also contact the Loan Consolidation Information Call Center at 1-800-557-7392, or visit http://www.studentloans.gov for more information. Parents may even be eligible to consolidate Parent PLUS Loans.

Make sure you research the pros and cons of consolidation to see if it is a good option for you. Note that federal loans cannot be consolidated with private loans. Therefore, it is important to follow up with your loan servicer to see if this option is available.

Beware: When consolidating, do not fall for student loan scams! You do not have to pay ANY vendor to consolidate your loans! Watch out for these corporations that capitalize off of students who do not understand the student plan repayment process.

As I've said, students and graduates in the United States have a combined student loan debt of 1.3 trillion dollars. As a result, information from "student debt relief" companies are being mailed and promoted to recent graduates, promising to eliminate, consolidate, or lower student loan payments *for a fee*.

You may also have seen advertisements of student debt relief companies on social media, seemingly endorsed by celebrities who are paid to advertise the services of student debt relief companies on their Instagram accounts.

These companies' marketing materials suggest that they are affiliated with the federal government. **They are not!**

The truth is that companies that claim to eliminate, consolidate, or lower your student loan payments cannot change the terms of your loan in *any way*. These companies are not a quick fix! In some cases, they will put you further in debt.

Typically, these third-party companies begin to contact you during your six-month grace period.

Everyday lenders are calling graduates, yet account holders (graduates) are ignoring their lenders. However, graduates will call a third-party company that they saw on their favorite celebrity's Instagram page. And before they know it, they're scammed out of hundreds of dollars.

Please note: Federal student loans can only be consolidated through the Federal Direct Consolidation Program.

Oftentimes, these third-party programs will do nothing for you, yet take your money . . . because you provided them your bank account information to directly withdraw from your account.

There is no such thing as eliminating your student debt or companies offering you lower interest rates for a fee.

The majority of student loans are borrowed from the federal government. The Department of Education offers a variety of payment options that meet your needs and will work for you. Yet, in order to be eligible for these services, you must call them and begin to build a relationship with your loan servicer. Building a positive relationship with your lender will ensure that you will achieve all your financial goals.

Remember, if you choose to ignore your lender, they have the power to garnish your tax refunds and paychecks until your debt is completely paid in full. It is not what you owe, but who you owe! So be sure to protect yourself, and do not sign up for third-party "student debt relief" companies.

Some students **refinance** *private* loans to help lower their monthly payments. You may qualify for an interest rate discount. However, please take note of how much of your payments go to the principal and interest, so you can decide whether refinancing is the right option for you.

With all the information you've now accumulated, you should be able to pursue your college dream successfully and manage the big payoff of your college debt.

✓ If you have any questions or would like to consult with me personally about financing a college education for yourself or your child, I would be happy to assist you. Simply contact me via www.collegegurl.com.

Glossary

Adjusted Gross Income (AGI). You and/or your
family's total gross income minus specific deductions.

award package. Package provided by your prospective school
that includes the total amount of federal and non-federal
financial awards for the year. Additionally, it will show
projected out-of-pocket expense for the academic year.

borrower. A person who borrows money under an agreement
that it will be paid back.

Cost of Attendance (COA). The estimated total costs of
college for a single year, which includes direct and indirect
expenses: tuition, books, room and board, travel, and the
like. Cost of Attendance plays a major role in your award
package given by the institution, as it determines how much
aid you may be eligible for.

consolidation. Process of merging multiple loans into one
loan.

credit score. A number that represents a person's creditworthiness.

deferment. A period where your payments are temporarily
postponed.

default. The act of neglecting financial debts.

dependency status. To qualify for federal and state aid, you
must know whose information you will report on your Free
Application for Federal Student Aid (FAFSA). If you are a
dependent student, you must report your earnings as well as
that of your parents or guardians. If you are an independent

student, you will only report your own information (if married you will include your spouse's earnings) on the FAFSA. Dependency status will be based on your answers to questions 46 to 58 on the FAFSA.

disbursement. Funds that are paid out.

endorser. Someone who agrees to pay the loan if the borrower does not.

entrance counseling. A requirement given to first-time borrowers to understand the terms and conditions of the Federal Direct Loan Program.

exit counseling. A requirement administered when students drop below half-time and/or leave school that provides important information for repaying federal loans.

Expected Family Contribution (EFC). The information you submit on the FAFSA enables the government to determine your Expected Family Contribution—how much you should contribute to your or your child's education. The government takes into account adjusted gross income, household size, and assets to determine if you are eligible for need-based aid.

Family Education Rights and Privacy Act (FERPA). Protects the release of student records and information.

Federal Work-Study (FWS) Program. Provides part-time employment through the institution for financially needy students.

financial aid. Money given to offset educational expenses. Financial aid comes in various forms: scholarships, grants, loans, and work-study.

forbearance. The period during which your monthly payments are temporarily reduced or suspended. To qualify for forbearance, you must show the lender proof of financial hardship. Additionally, the interest that accrues during this period will be added to the overall principle balance even though payments are postponed.

Free Application for Federal Student Aid (FAFSA). Helps determine the awarding of federal and state aid. The FAFSA is the first step in seeking a post-secondary education and requires you and/or your family to provide your financial information. This information will determine how much aid the student may qualify for.

FSA ID. Identification username/password that provides access to all federal student aid databases (i.e., FAFSA.ed.gov, NSLDS.ed.gov, and studentloans.gov).

grace period. A six-month period during which you do not have to make a payment to the loan servicer. This period occurs after you leave school or drop below half-time status.

grant. Free money given by federal and/or state governments, organizations, and institutions to offset college expenses. Some grants may be based on financial need, while others may be based on other criteria.

interest. Fee charged from the lender to the borrower for the life of the loan.

IRS Data Retrieval Tool (DRT). Allows students and parents to electronically link their tax information to the FAFSA. It is recommended students and parents utilize this tool for accuracy to ensure that your Expected Family Contribution (EFC) is accurate.

loans. Money borrowed by federal and private lenders that must be paid back with interest.

Master Promissory Note (MPN). A legal document where you agree to repay your loans, interests, and fees to the

U.S. Department of Education.

merit-based aid. Financial award that is based on academic performance, athletic ability, special skills, and/or interests. Families who do not qualify for need-based aid may be eligible to qualify for merit-based aid.

National Student Loan Data System (NSLDS). A database operated by the U.S. Department of Education to keeps track of your federal student loan history.

need-based aid. Aid that is determined by you or your family's annual income; the annual income your family makes and members within the household will determine if you are eligible for need-based aid.

Pell Grant. Need-based aid granted by the federal government for students with a strong financial need, which is determined by the family's income, size, and assets.

Public Service Loan Forgiveness (PSLF). Forgives the remaining balance on loans once you have made 120 on-time payments on your payment plan if you work within the field of public service.

refinance. The process of modifying payments to secure a lower interest rate.

refund. When your financial aid exceeds the charges on your student account, it will generate a refund.

repayment. The amount of funds borrowed that must be repaid to the lender.

Satisfactory Academic Progress (SAP). The established grade point average (GPA) you must maintain to continue to be eligible for federal, state, and institutional aid. If you are an undergrad you must maintain a minimum of a 2.0 GPA. If you are a graduate student you must maintain a minimum of a 3.0 GPA.

scholarship. A grant awarded to a student based on academic performance, athletic ability, special skills, and/or interests that does not need to be repaid.

Student Aid Report (SAR). The result of the FAFSA that shows your eligibility for student aid.

subsidized loans. Loans awarded based on financial need where the federal government pays the interest on the loan while the student is enrolled at least part-time.

Teacher Loan Forgiveness. Must enter into the teaching profession for five years to receive forgiveness up to $17,500.

unsubsidized loans. Non-need-based loans where interest accrues once the loan is disbursed to the student's account.

About the Author

As a financial aid administrator at multiple post-secondary institutions, Jessica L. Brown has assisted students, parents, and guardians to successfully navigate the seas of financial aid. Her exhaustive knowledge and understanding of both college financing opportunities and financing pitfalls has benefitted countless individuals.

Now founder and CEO of College Gurl, Jessica has expanded her reach to a larger audience through www.collegegurl.com, an online resource to increase financial literacy among post-secondary students and their families.

In addition, she is National Spokesperson of College Financing for the dfree® Financial Freedom Movement. dfree® is a transformational lifestyle movement that promotes financial freedom through values-based principles and practical approaches to financial management.

Jessica's mission is to ensure that students have a secure financial future after graduation and that parents/guardians are well informed about the programs, policies, and strategies that result in making the best-informed decisions around their children's college education.

Jessica received a BA in Broadcast Journalism from Howard University's John H. Johnson School of Communications and Masters of Science Management from Strayer University.

Contact Jessica L. Brown via www.collegegurl.com.

CPSIA information can be obtained
at www.ICGtesting.com
Printed in the USA
BVOW06s0727040617

485987BV00015B/991/P